York's Green Places

Compiled by Judith Ward

Edited by Dave Meigh, Mick Phythian, Bill Sessions & Elizabeth Smith

Additional information supplied by
City of York Council, York Natural Environment Trust,
Yorkshire Wildlife Trust & Friends or management groups
of the following Green Places:
Acomb Wood, Beech Grove, Chapman's Pond, Clifton Backies,
Danesmead Meadow, Fishponds Wood, Hagg Wood,
Hassacarr Nature Reserve, Heworth Holme, Hob Moor,
Mayfield Nature Reserve, New Earswick Nature Reserves,
St. Nicholas Fields, Wheatlands Educational Community Woodland,
West Bank Park, York Cemetery.

Sessions Book Trust
The Ebor Press
York, England

ISBN 1 85072 352 4

The front cover of the Millennium Bridge is reproduced by courtesy of the York artist Brenda Tyler © 11 Sandringham Street, York

Grateful acknowledgement is made for the financial support of
The Sessions Book Trust, City of York Council
and English Nature

The Publishers will be pleased to receive additional and updated information

On page 3 the photo of Heworth Holme in snow is by Ted Hughes, and the others are by Lisa Pickering.

Printed by
Sessions of York
The Ebor Press
York, England

York's Green Places

Aerial photographs show York as a remarkably green city. Over the centuries, built-up areas have enveloped ancient strays and commons, woods and riverside meadows. Some parts of this landscape have been tamed and civilised, as parks, playgrounds, promenades and gardens. Others are little changed; remnants of old countryside woven into the urban fabric.

Green pathways on the Bar Walls (above) and north along the River Ouse (below)

Some of these green places now lie alongside main roads, obvious to passers-by, but others are hidden away behind the buildings of the modern city. Newcomers or visitors to the city are likely to pass these places by without knowing of their existence. Lifelong residents can still be surprised by a hidden green place, overlooked for years.

Many of York's green places are linked into green corridors, along the two main rivers or their many tributaries, and along old footpaths or half-forgotten lanes. Linked spaces have extra value as wildlife habitats. They also offer attractive green routes for human users, on foot or bicycle, and a chance to step back from the 21st century.

Snow on Heworth Holme

A veteran beech tree in Moorlands Wood

Sculpture in York Cemetery

This guide invites you to discover some of York's green places for yourself. It includes details of over forty sites ranging from riverside promenades and Edwardian parks to ancient meadows, woods and wetlands. Some are rural nature reserves in the green belt around the city, but these are not the only places which offer a taste of the countryside. You can enjoy the song of larks, the chirping of grasshoppers or the colour and scent of bluebells less than a mile from the bar walls. You just need to know where to look.

Finding York's Green Places - alphabetical list & reference map

1 Acomb Green
2 Acomb Wood
3 Askham Bog
4 Bachelor Hill
5 Beech Grove
6 Bootham Stray
7 Chapman's Pond
8 City Centre
9 Clarence Gardens
10 Clifton Backies

11 Clifton Ings
12 Danesmead Meadow
13 Fishponds Wood
14 Fulford Ings
15 Glen Gardens
16 Hagg Wood
17 Hassacarr Pond

18 Heslington Common
19 Heworth Holme
20 Heworth Stray
21 Hob Moor

22 Homestead Park
23 Hull Road Park
24 Knavesmire

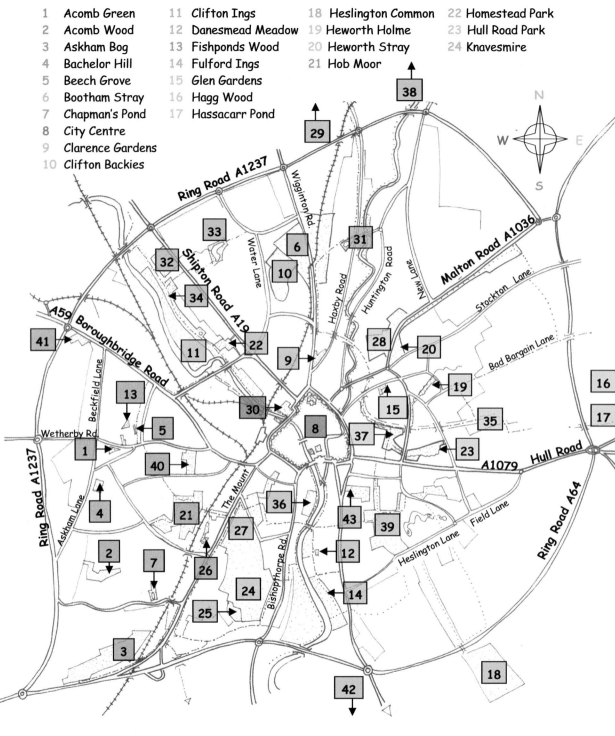

25 Knavesmire Wood
26 Mayfield
27 Micklegate Stray
28 Monk Stray
29 Moorlands

30 Museum Gardens
31 New Earswick
32 Rawcliffe Bar
33 Rawcliffe Lake
34 Rawcliffe Meadows

35 Route 66 Cycle Track
36 Rowntree Park
37 St. Nicholas Fields
38 Strensall Common
39 Walmgate Stray

40 West Bank Park
41 Wheatlands
42 Wheldrake Ings
43 York Cemetery

Using this Guide

The reference map will help you to find green places in a particular part of York or to check the location of a place you know by name. There are thirty pages of sketch maps with detailed information for individual sites. These are arranged in four sections: north (from page 6), east (from page 16), south (from page 26) and west of the city (from page 34) with a centre spread covering the many small green spaces in the city centre.

Getting Around

Most of the green places in this guide are easily accessible by public transport, on foot or by bicycle. Bus information is given as an indication of routes and services but should be checked, by phoning one of the numbers given below. Car parking information is given for those who need it. If you use a car out of choice rather than necessity, consider leaving it at home and using another means of transport. You'll be contributing to the health of York's wider environment, and you'll have a chance to discover some extra green places along your way.

For bus time table information contact
Traveline (all services) : 0870 608 2 608   www.traveline.org.uk
First York: 01904 551400   www.firstgroup.com
Yorkshire Coastliner: 01653 692556   www.yorkshirecoastliner.co.uk

Getting Involved

Many of York's green places are cared for by volunteer Friends groups. Some groups are involved in management planning, wildlife recording, special events or work with schools. Others take responsibility for some or all of the day-to-day maintenance of a site. A number of Friends groups come under the umbrella of York Natural Environment Trust (YNET), a group which aims to conserve, protect and enhance the natural environment of York. British Trust for Conservation Volunteers (BTCV) undertake practical tasks on nature reserves and other green sites. Yorkshire Wildlife Trust (YWT) reserves are maintained with the assistance of volunteers. Both BTCV and YWT also run environmental activities for children and young people.

For general information on parks and open spaces in York contact
City of York Council
Parks and Open Spaces Section : 01904 613161 www.york.gov.uk/leisure/parks

For information on YNET and a number of Friends groups visit
York Communigate website: www.communigate.co.uk/york

For information on YWT Reserves contact
Yorkshire Wildlife Trust: 01904 659570   www.yorkshire-wildlife-trust.org.uk

For information on conservation volunteering contact
BTCV Vale of York group: 01904 644300   www.btcv.org/users/york

Green Places in North York

North west from the city centre along the River Ouse and due north along the River Foss, foo paths and cycle ways link two chains of peaceful green places.   The green wedge of Bootham Stray is another remnant of historic countryside within the fabric of the modern city.

Bootham Stray

Grid Reference: SE 562 545   Open access.   Informal paths, wet and muddy in winter.
Held in trust by City of York Council. Managed by CoYC in consultation with the Freemen of the City.

More than 100 acres of grassland, mostly grazed by cattle all year round.

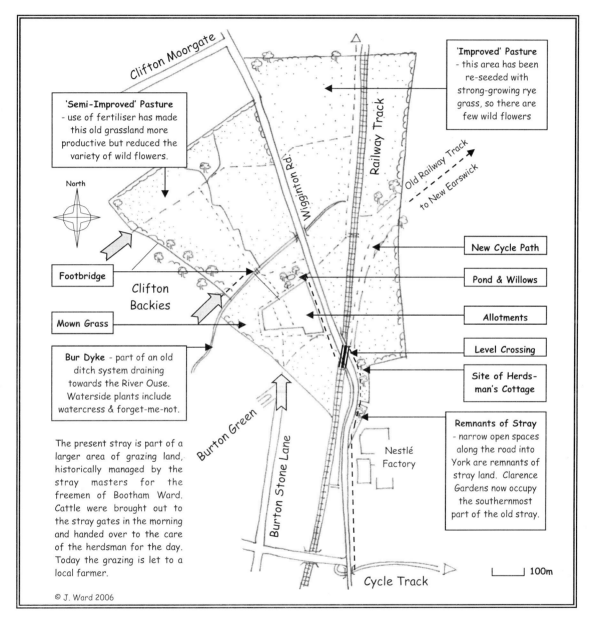

'Improved' Pasture
- this area has been re-seeded with strong-growing rye grass, so there are few wild flowers

'Semi-Improved' Pasture
- use of fertiliser has made this old grassland more productive but reduced the variety of wild flowers.

North

Footbridge

Clifton Backies

Mown Grass

Bur Dyke - part of an old ditch system draining towards the River Ouse. Waterside plants include watercress & forget-me-not.

The present stray is part of a larger area of grazing land, historically managed by the stray masters for the freemen of Bootham Ward. Cattle were brought out to the stray gates in the morning and handed over to the care of the herdsman for the day. Today the grazing is let to a local farmer.

© J. Ward 2006

Clifton Moorgate

Wigginton Rd.

Railway Track

Old Railway Track to New Earswick

New Cycle Path

Pond & Willows

Allotments

Level Crossing

Site of Herdsman's Cottage

Remnants of Stray
- narrow open spaces along the road into York are remnants of stray land. Clarence Gardens now occupy the southernmost part of the old stray.

Burton Green

Burton Stone Lane

Nestlé Factory

Cycle Track

100m

Bootham Stray is an important part of the historic landscape of York and a link to the surrounding farmland. There's a great sense of space but the busy Wigginton Road, cutting through the stray, makes this piece of countryside in the town feel less peaceful than it looks.

Bus: First York 6 to Burton Stone Lane / Burton Green corner.

Clarence Gardens

Grid Reference: SE 604 529.   Open 8.00 a.m. to dusk.
Managed by City of York Council in association with Clarence Gardens Bowling Association.

These small, traditional public gardens, enclosed by mature trees, offer a breathing space in a busy urban setting. There are three bowling greens, rose beds and plenty of benches in the main part of the gardens. The well-equipped children's play area is on the opposite side of the entrance to the car park. The gardens occupy the southern tip of the old Bootham Stray.

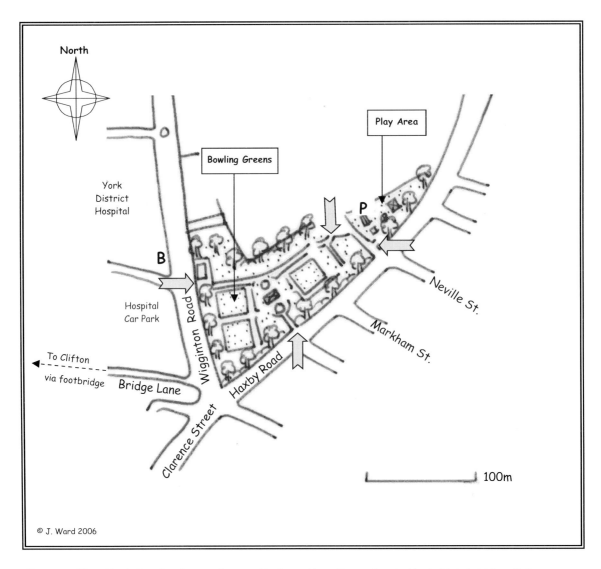

Buses: First York Service 6 runs frequently from the city centre to York District Hospital.

Parking: There is a small pay & display car park adjacent to the gardens. Access from Haxby Road.

Clifton Backies Local Nature Reserve

Grid Reference: SE 596 545.   Open access.   Main paths level and well surfaced.
Leased to City of York Council.   Managed by Clifton Backies Management Board.

This area has seen varied use over the centuries, from arable fields in monastic times to an airfield in World War II.   Surviving historic features include the ridges and furrows created by medieval ox ploughs and the concrete airfield paths that provide level access today.

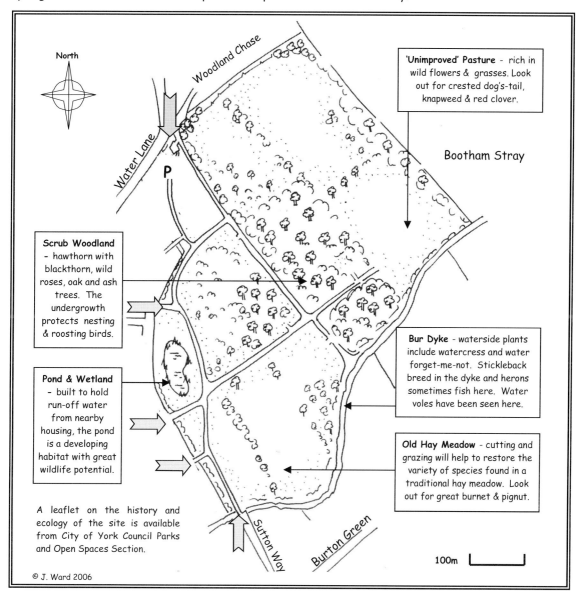

North

Woodland Chase

Water Lane

P

'Unimproved' Pasture - rich in wild flowers & grasses. Look out for crested dog's-tail, knapweed & red clover.

Bootham Stray

Scrub Woodland - hawthorn with blackthorn, wild roses, oak and ash trees. The undergrowth protects nesting & roosting birds.

Bur Dyke - waterside plants include watercress and water forget-me-not. Stickleback breed in the dyke and herons sometimes fish here. Water voles have been seen here.

Pond & Wetland - built to hold run-off water from nearby housing, the pond is a developing habitat with great wildlife potential.

Old Hay Meadow - cutting and grazing will help to restore the variety of species found in a traditional hay meadow. Look out for great burnet & pignut.

A leaflet on the history and ecology of the site is available from City of York Council Parks and Open Spaces Section.

Sutton Way

Burton Green

100m

© J. Ward 2006

The three major habitat types of Clifton Backies, unimproved pasture, scrub woodland and unimproved hay meadow, support many bird species. In summer several different species of warblers can be heard singing. In winter large numbers of blackbirds, fieldfares and redwings feed on the hawthorn berries.

Bus: First York 6 runs frequently from the city centre to Water Lane.
Parking: Small car park reached from Woodland Chase.

The River Ouse Corridor - North of the City

The green corridor alongside the River Ouse includes a wide variety of open spaces, ranging from ornamental gardens and playing fields to flower-rich meadows and a country park. A walk or bike ride north from the city centre, on the east bank of the river, offers an unrivalled selection of green places, each with a different character.

Starting from the Park & Ride car park or bus stops, a 3 mile walk leads through a chain of linked green places to the Yorkshire Museum Gardens (see page 24). Buses back to Rawcliffe Bar leave Museum Street, outside the entrance to the Gardens, frequently throughout the day.

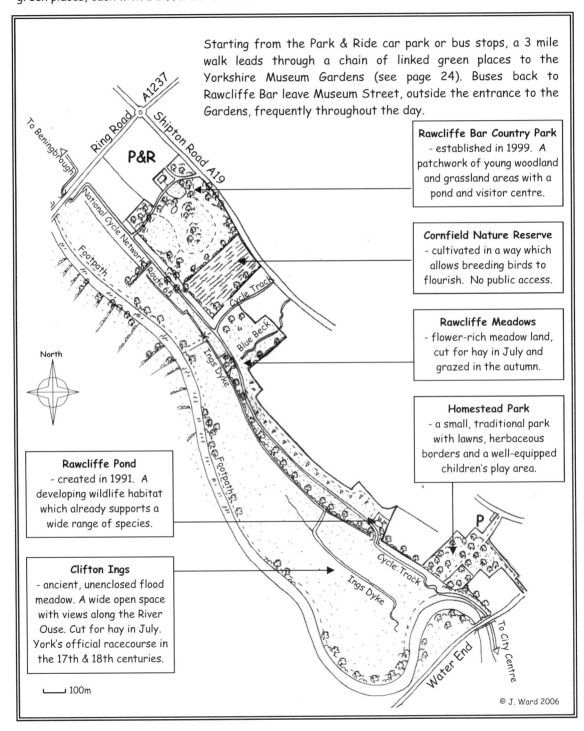

Rawcliffe Bar Country Park
- established in 1999. A patchwork of young woodland and grassland areas with a pond and visitor centre.

Cornfield Nature Reserve
- cultivated in a way which allows breeding birds to flourish. No public access.

Rawcliffe Meadows
- flower-rich meadow land, cut for hay in July and grazed in the autumn.

Homestead Park
- a small, traditional park with lawns, herbaceous borders and a well-equipped children's play area.

Rawcliffe Pond
- created in 1991. A developing wildlife habitat which already supports a wide range of species.

Clifton Ings
- ancient, unenclosed flood meadow. A wide open space with views along the River Ouse. Cut for hay in July. York's official racecourse in the 17th & 18th centuries.

100m

© J. Ward 2006

10

Rawcliffe Bar Country Park

Grid Reference: SE 577 547   Open access.   Informal paths and mown grass access.
Owned and Managed by City of York Council.   Toilets at Park and Ride.

Some 2000 trees and 1,500 woodland shrubs were planted during the establishment of the Country Park. Developing woodland includes willow, birch and pine with oak and ash. Hawthorn, blackthorn and dog rose thickets give nesting cover and food for an increasing range of birds. The Visitor Centre is the focus for activity days and special events and can be booked for use by school parties. Contact City of York Council Parks and Open Spaces Section on York 613161 for details.

Cornfield Nature Reserve

Grid Reference: SE 578 543   No public access.   11 acres
Owned by City of York Council.   Managed under a DEFRA Countryside Stewardship agreement.

Cereal crops grown on this land are spring sown in the traditional manner, leaving the stubble of the previous crop to provide food and cover for birds over the winter. Ground-nesting birds, including skylarks and grey partridge, are sheltered by the growing crop.

Rawcliffe Meadows

Grid Reference: SE 585 534   Open Access.   Sustrans cycle path runs through the meadow.
Owned by the Environment Agency. Managed by Friends of Rawcliffe Meadows.   25 acres.

Before 1991 the meadows had suffered from over-grazing for many years. Since that date, the Friends of Rawcliffe Meadow have re-established traditional hay meadow stewardship with seasonal grazing after an annual hay harvest, allowing wildflowers to flower and set seed, attracting butterflies and birds. The meadows are particularly beautiful in early summer when lady's smock, meadowsweet and great burnet flower, among drifts of buttercups. Old hedgerows and two small copses provide safe habitats for may different species of birds and small mammals.

Clifton Ings

Grid Reference: SE 585 530   Open Access   Informal footpath along the riverside.

Around 80 acres of land in seven different ownerships, a legacy of the medieval Lammas system. Lammas Lands were opened to common grazing once the owners had harvested the hay. A wide range of wild flowers thrive on the Ings, adapted to this pattern of management. Please keep to the footpath if the hay has not yet been cut.

Homestead Park

Grid Reference: SE 588 531   Open from 9.00 a.m. to dusk.   No access from riverside.
Owned and managed by the Joseph Rowntree Foundation.
Pedestrian access from Water End and Shipton Road. Small car park at Shipton Road entrance.

Avenues and groups of ornamental trees give spring blossom and autumn colour. This well-maintained park is a popular place for family picnics. For more information contact JRF on (01904) 629241.

Moorlands Nature Reserve

Grid Reference: SE 580 587   Owned and managed by Yorkshire Wildlife Trust.
Open access with level pathways. Please keep to the paths. No dogs except guide dogs.

An 18 acre mixed woodland, developed in the early 20th century as a woodland garden, Moorlands provides sheltered habitats for a wide variety of wildlife: over 50 species of birds have been recorded. Snowdrops, daffodils, bluebells, rhododendrons and maples give seasonal colour from February through to the autumn.

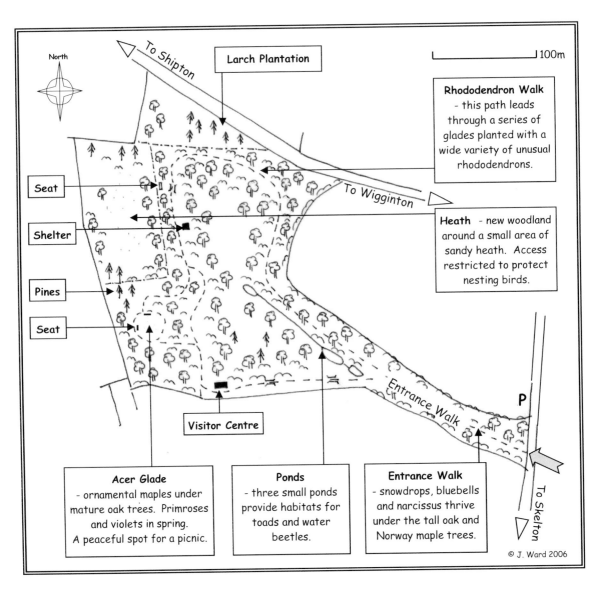

North

To Shipton

Larch Plantation

100m

Rhododendron Walk
- this path leads through a series of glades planted with a wide variety of unusual rhododendrons.

To Wigginton

Heath - new woodland around a small area of sandy heath. Access restricted to protect nesting birds.

Seat

Shelter

Pines

Seat

Entrance Walk

P

To Skelton

Visitor Centre

Acer Glade
- ornamental maples under mature oak trees. Primroses and violets in spring.
A peaceful spot for a picnic.

Ponds
- three small ponds provide habitats for toads and water beetles.

Entrance Walk
- snowdrops, bluebells and narcissus thrive under the tall oak and Norway maple trees.

© J. Ward 2006

Moorlands is about five miles north of York city centre. There is no bus service to the reserve.
By bike: Take the Haxby Road, which has a cycle underpass crossing the A1237 ring road. Turn left in Haxby to Wigginton, right at the B1363 then left towards Shipton & left at the next crossroads.
By car: Take A19 to Skelton. Turn right off A19 through village, then continue 2 miles to reserve.

Rawcliffe Lake

Grid Reference: SE 587 546

Owned and Managed by City of York Council.   Open access.   Tarmac paths.

Grassy slopes and developing wildlife areas around a 7 acre artificial lake, created in the 1980s.

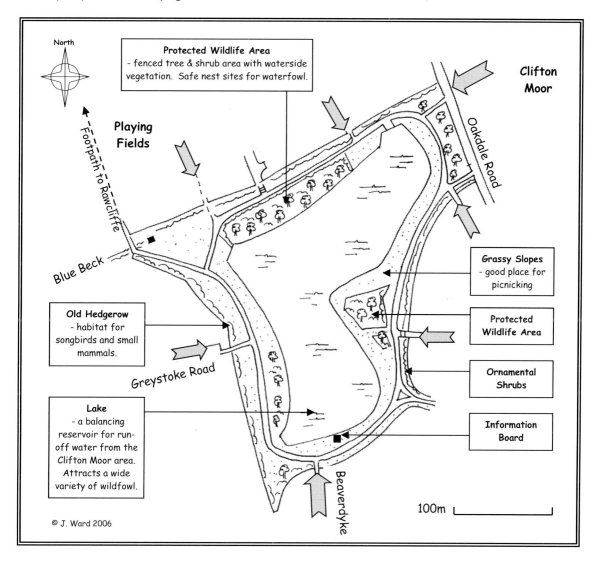

North

Protected Wildlife Area
- fenced tree & shrub area with waterside vegetation. Safe nest sites for waterfowl.

Clifton Moor

Oakdale Road

Footpath to Rawcliffe

Playing Fields

Blue Beck

Grassy Slopes
- good place for picnicking

Old Hedgerow
- habitat for songbirds and small mammals.

Greystoke Road

Protected Wildlife Area

Ornamental Shrubs

Lake
- a balancing reservoir for run-off water from the Clifton Moor area. Attracts a wide variety of wildfowl.

Information Board

Beaverdyke

100m

© J. Ward 2006

Buses: First York 6 from City Centre to Oakdale Road.

By Bike: Take Sustrans route north along River Ouse to Rawcliffe access. Cross A19 and follow Loweswater Road, Westholme Drive and Eastholme Drive to Greystoke Road. No cycling on the site.

By Car: Follow Rawcliffe Lane from Clifton. At Eastholme Drive roundabout keep right into Green Lane, then first left to Beaverdyke. Limited on-street parking. Please park with consideration for local residents.

Fishing: Managed by York and District Amalgamation of Anglers (YDAA). All anglers must hold a current permit to fish in the lake. Further information from YDAA General Secretary at St. Clements Club, Count de Burgh Terrace, York YO23 1HH or from City of York Council Parks and Open Spaces Section.

New Earswick Nature Reserves & River Foss

Grid Reference: SE 608 548 (Brick Pond) / SE 610 547 (Lock Island)

Co-operation between a number of different groups and land owners has secured the future of a chain of small nature reserves along the wildlife corridor of the River Foss and Old Foss Beck. The protected habitats in these reserves provide safe breeding grounds for birds and other wildlife, glimpsed from the attractive footpaths along the River Foss and the old railway track.

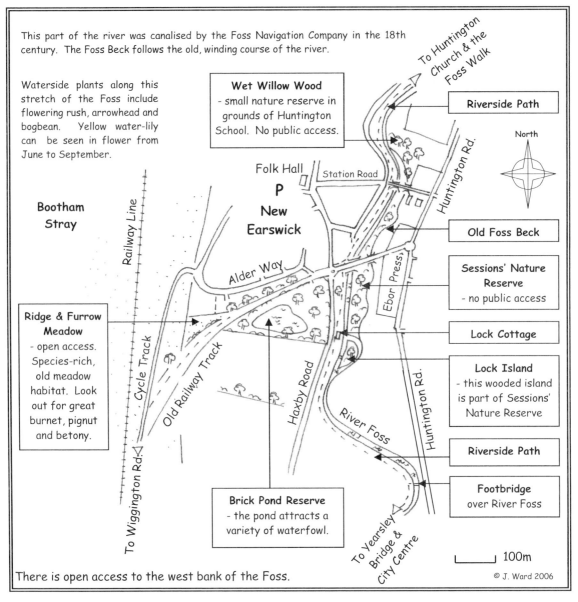

This part of the river was canalised by the Foss Navigation Company in the 18th century. The Foss Beck follows the old, winding course of the river.

To Huntington Church & the Foss Walk

Waterside plants along this stretch of the Foss include flowering rush, arrowhead and bogbean. Yellow water-lily can be seen in flower from June to September.

Wet Willow Wood
- small nature reserve in grounds of Huntington School. No public access.

Riverside Path

North

Bootham Stray

Railway Line

Folk Hall
P
New Earswick

Station Road

Huntington Rd.

Old Foss Beck

Alder Way

Ebor Press

Sessions' Nature Reserve
- no public access

Ridge & Furrow Meadow
- open access. Species-rich, old meadow habitat. Look out for great burnet, pignut and betony.

Cycle Track

Old Railway Track

Haxby Road

Lock Cottage

Lock Island
- this wooded island is part of Sessions' Nature Reserve

Huntington Rd.

River Foss

Riverside Path

Footbridge over River Foss

To Wiggington Rd.

Brick Pond Reserve
- the pond attracts a variety of waterfowl.

To Yearsley Bridge & City Centre

└─────┘ 100m

There is open access to the west bank of the Foss.

© J. Ward 2006

To visit the Brick Pond Nature Reserve, apply for a key to Joseph Rowntree Housing Trust, Tanners Yard, Huntington Road, York. An illustrated book 'New Earswick Nature Reserve: the First Half Century' is available from Sessions Printers, Huntington Road, York.

Buses: First York Services 1 & 2 run regularly along the Haxby Road, stopping at the Folk Hall.

Strensall Common Nature Reserve

Grid Reference: SE 647 615
Owned and managed by Yorkshire Wildlife Trust.

Open access on public / permissive footpaths.
Dogs must be kept under close control.

41 hectares of richly varied lowland heath with many seasonal ponds. The reserve is part of a larger area of heath known as Strensall Common, although it is no longer open common land.

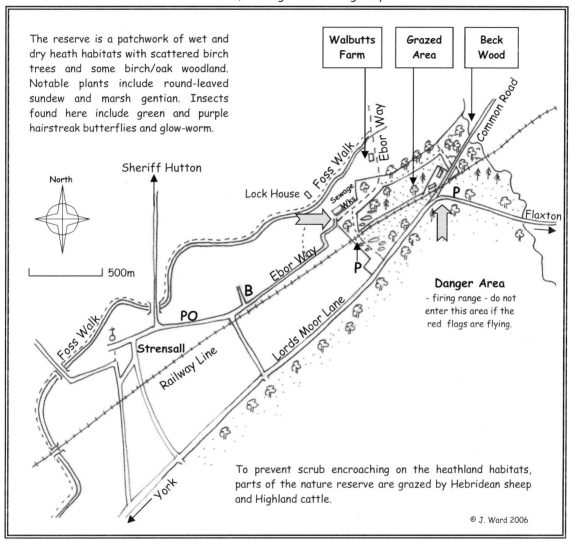

The reserve is a patchwork of wet and dry heath habitats with scattered birch trees and some birch/oak woodland. Notable plants include round-leaved sundew and marsh gentian. Insects found here include green and purple hairstreak butterflies and glow-worm.

Danger Area
- firing range - do not enter this area if the red flags are flying.

To prevent scrub encroaching on the heathland habitats, parts of the nature reserve are grazed by Hebridean sheep and Highland cattle.

© J. Ward 2006

Foss Walk

The Foss Walk follows the riverside for 8 miles from York to Strensall. A permissive path, from Lock House to Walbutts Farm, allows the walk to link up with the Ebor Way just north of Strensall Common. For details of the route north of Strensall, see 'The Foss Walk' by Mark Jones, published by Maxiprint.

Buses: Strensall is served by frequent buses. From the terminus of First York service 5 (at **B**) the Ebor Way follows the (almost) traffic-free Brecks Lane to the reserve entrance.

By Car: From York, turn right to Flaxton before reaching the centre of Strensall. Turn into the lane on your left, just after the cattle grid or continue to the Common Road rail crossing. Don't take cars over the crossing.

Green Places in East York

Two small tributaries of the River Foss flow through East York: the Tang Hall Beck and the Osbaldwick Beck. Each beck runs in a narrow green corridor, until they disappear into underground culverts. The two watercourses now meet underground in St. Nicholas Fields, at the 'tang' or fork which gave Tang Hall its name. The Foss Islands Cycle Track forms another green link out of the city centre.

Glen Gardens

Grid Reference: SE 615 525   Owned and managed by City of York Council.
Open from 9.00 a.m. to dusk daily.   No cycling allowed in the Gardens.

A traditional, neighbourhood park on Heworth's main street, one mile east of York city centre. Glen Gardens has bowling greens, tennis courts, a rose garden and a well-equipped children's play area.

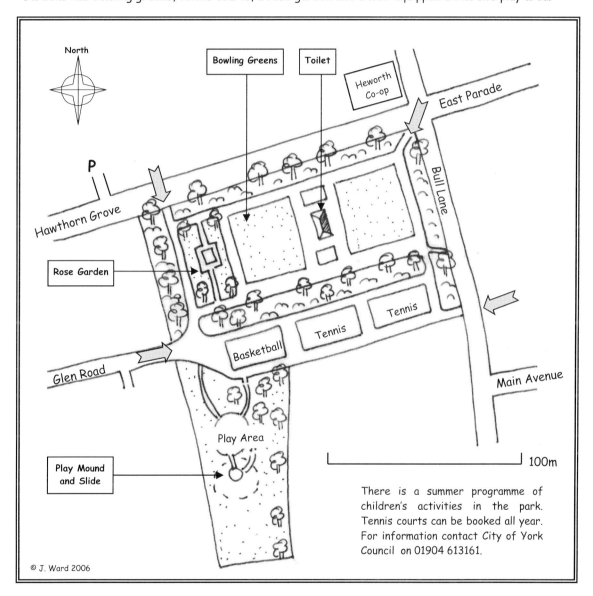

There is a summer programme of children's activities in the park. Tennis courts can be booked all year. For information contact City of York Council on 01904 613161.

© J. Ward 2006

Buses: First York Service 6 runs frequently from the city centre to Glen Road. First 11 and 13 and Yorkshire Coastliner services run regularly along East Parade, stopping outside Heworth Co-op.

By Bike: The Foss Islands cycle route crosses Hawthorn Grove just west of the park.

Parking: There is a small car park on the opposite side of East Parade.

Heworth Holme

Grid Reference: SE 622 526.   Open Access.   Informal paths can be wet or muddy in winter.
Owned by City of York Council   Managed by City of York Council and Friends of Heworth Holme.

Six acres of wet grassland alongside the Tang Hall Beck, and a small wood on higher ground.

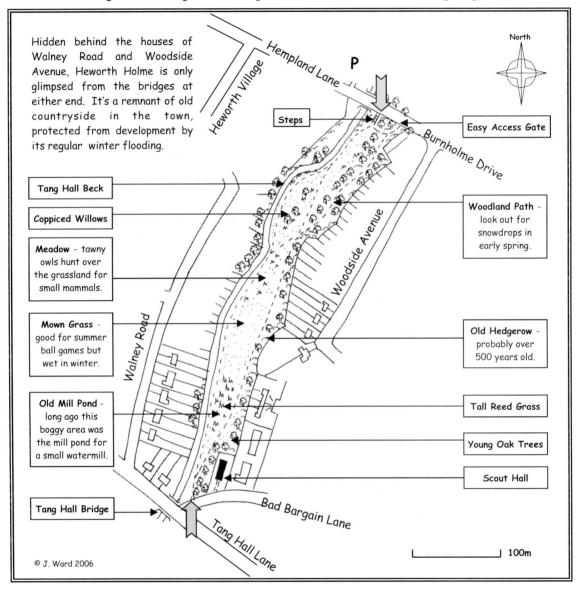

Hidden behind the houses of Walney Road and Woodside Avenue, Heworth Holme is only glimpsed from the bridges at either end. It's a remnant of old countryside in the town, protected from development by its regular winter flooding.

North

P

Hempland Lane

Heworth Village

Steps

Easy Access Gate

Burnholme Drive

Tang Hall Beck

Coppiced Willows

Meadow - tawny owls hunt over the grassland for small mammals.

Mown Grass - good for summer ball games but wet in winter.

Old Mill Pond - long ago this boggy area was the mill pond for a small watermill.

Tang Hall Bridge

Walney Road

Woodside Avenue

Woodland Path - look out for snowdrops in early spring.

Old Hedgerow - probably over 500 years old.

Tall Reed Grass

Young Oak Trees

Scout Hall

Bad Bargain Lane

Tang Hall Lane

100m

© J. Ward 2006

40 species of birds have been recorded here. Kingfishers sometimes fish in the beck and water vole have been seen. In spring great spotted woodpeckers can be heard drumming on hollow trees.

By Bus: First York 13 to Heworth Village or 11 to Tang Hall Lane.
Parking: There is a small car park at the Hempland Lane allotments, across the road from the Holme.

Monk Stray

Grid Reference: SE 616 534   Open access to part only.   Informal paths.
Managed by City of York Council in consultation with Freeman of the City.

The remnants of the historic Monk Stray are divided into four distinct areas: the grassy parkland known as Heworth Stray, two areas of rough grazing land to either side of the Malton Road, and the privately leased golf course. Open views in towards York Minster & out to surrounding countryside.

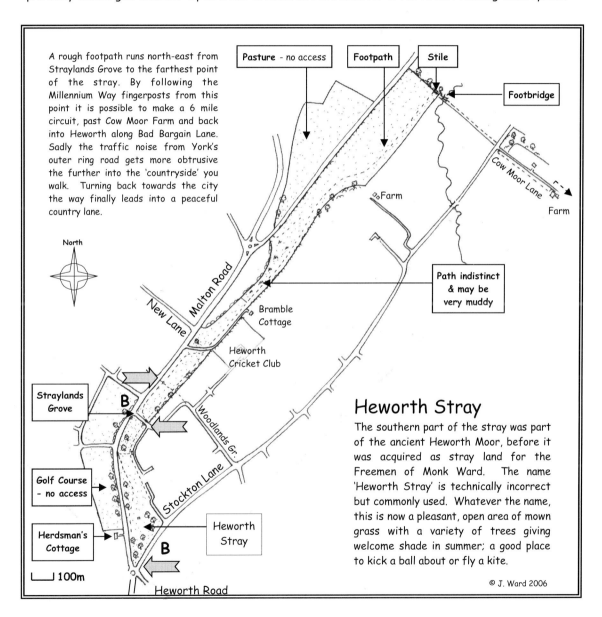

A rough footpath runs north-east from Straylands Grove to the farthest point of the stray. By following the Millennium Way fingerposts from this point it is possible to make a 6 mile circuit, past Cow Moor Farm and back into Heworth along Bad Bargain Lane. Sadly the traffic noise from York's outer ring road gets more obtrusive the further into the 'countryside' you walk. Turning back towards the city the way finally leads into a peaceful country lane.

North

Pasture - no access

Footpath

Stile

Footbridge

Cow Moor Lane

Farm

Farm

Path indistinct & may be very muddy

Malton Road

New Lane

Bramble Cottage

Heworth Cricket Club

Straylands Grove

B

Woodlands Gr.

Stockton Lane

Golf Course - no access

Herdsman's Cottage

B

Heworth Stray

100m

Heworth Road

Heworth Stray

The southern part of the stray was part of the ancient Heworth Moor, before it was acquired as stray land for the Freemen of Monk Ward. The name 'Heworth Stray' is technically incorrect but commonly used. Whatever the name, this is now a pleasant, open area of mown grass with a variety of trees giving welcome shade in summer; a good place to kick a ball about or fly a kite.

© J. Ward 2006

Buses: First York 13 to Monk Stray (Elm Park Way) or Yorkshire Coastliner to Stockton Lane.
Parking: Unrestricted parking on most side streets in the area.

St. Nicholas Fields Local Nature Reserve

Grid Reference: SE 617 517.   Open Access with wheelchair-accessible paths.
Owned by City of York Council.   Managed by Friends of St. Nicholas Fields.   10 hectares.

In the Middles Ages this land was open fields, grazed by the cattle of the monks of St. Nicholas Hospital. Since then it's been a brick works, the city rubbish dump and an unofficial wild site. Now reclaimed and home to a wide range of species, developing habitats include meadows and woodland.

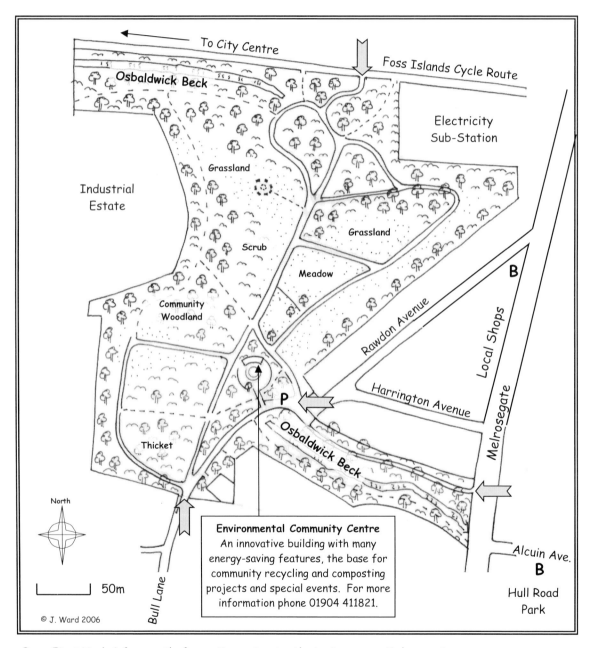

Bus: First York 6 frequently from city centre to Alcuin Avenue or Melrosegate.
Cycle/Pedestrian Entrances: From Foss Islands Cycle Route, or from Lawrence Street via Bull Lane.
Entrance to Small Car Park: From Melrosegate via Rawdon or Harrington Avenue.

20

Hull Road Park

Grid Reference: SE 623 636 Owned and Managed by City of York Council.
Open from 8.00 a.m. to dusk. Easy access with mostly level pathways.

A varied, traditional park, alongside the Osbaldwick Beck in Tang Hall, about one mile east of the city centre. A good place for ball games and picnics. St. Nicholas Fields is just across Melrosegate.

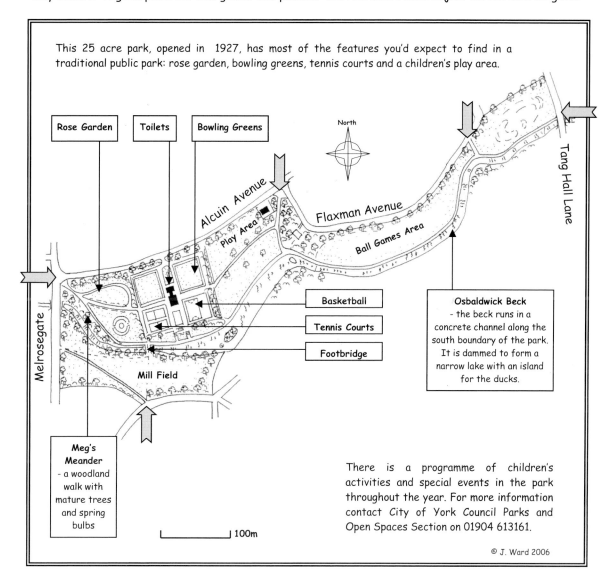

This 25 acre park, opened in 1927, has most of the features you'd expect to find in a traditional public park: rose garden, bowling greens, tennis courts and a children's play area.

Rose Garden

Toilets

Bowling Greens

North

Alcuin Avenue

Flaxman Avenue

Play Area

Ball Games Area

Tang Hall Lane

Melrosegate

Basketball

Tennis Courts

Footbridge

Mill Field

Osbaldwick Beck
- the beck runs in a concrete channel along the south boundary of the park. It is dammed to form a narrow lake with an island for the ducks.

Meg's Meander
- a woodland walk with mature trees and spring bulbs

100m

There is a programme of children's activities and special events in the park throughout the year. For more information contact City of York Council Parks and Open Spaces Section on 01904 613161.

© J. Ward 2006

Buses: First York Service 6 runs frequently from the city centre to Alcuin Avenue.

Cycle Route: Route 66 crosses both Melrosegate and Tang Hall Lane just north of the park.

Parking: Unrestricted on neighbouring streets.

Foss Islands Cycle Track - Route 66

This green route, managed by Sustrans, follows the route of the disused Derwent Valley Light Railway from Wigginton Road to Osbaldwick village. It's wheelchair accessible, though some of the entrance ramps are rather steep. The track provides habitat links for a wide range of garden birds, insects and small mammals. It's a good place to hear robins, wrens and thrushes singing.

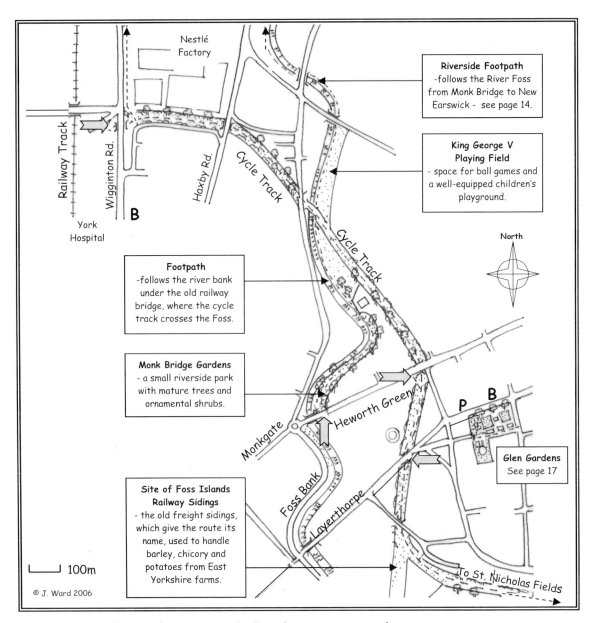

Nestlé Factory

Riverside Footpath
-follows the River Foss from Monk Bridge to New Earswick - see page 14.

King George V Playing Field
- space for ball games and a well-equipped children's playground.

Railway Track

Wigginton Rd.

York Hospital

B

Haxby Rd.

Cycle Track

Cycle Track

North

Footpath
-follows the river bank under the old railway bridge, where the cycle track crosses the Foss.

Monk Bridge Gardens
- a small riverside park with mature trees and ornamental shrubs.

Heworth Green

Monkgate

P   B

Glen Gardens
See page 17

Foss Bank

Layerthorpe

Site of Foss Islands Railway Sidings
- the old freight sidings, which give the route its name, used to handle barley, chicory and potatoes from East Yorkshire farms.

To St. Nicholas Fields

100m

© J. Ward 2006

The River Foss from Monk Bridge to Yearsley

The banks of York's second river are lined with willows along much of this stretch.
The informal path can be muddy and slippery in wet weather. In summer the trees give welcome shade. For links north and south along the river, see pages 15 and 25.

Hagg Wood

Grid Reference: SE 685 526.   Open Access.   Mostly level paths.
Owned by: Forest Enterprise.   Managed: in consultation with Friends of Hagg Wood.

100 acres of mixed woodland on an ancient woodland site, with bluebells, wood anemones and many other wild flowers. After a long campaign by local people, the wood was designated as a Community Woodland in May 2003, securing public access for future generations.

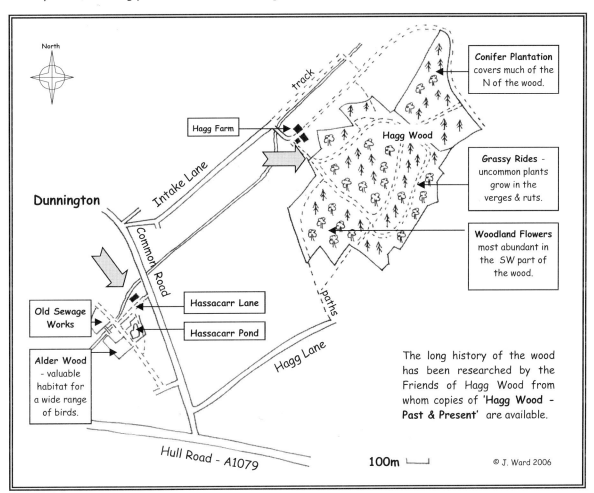

North

Conifer Plantation
covers much of the
N of the wood.

track

Hagg Farm

Hagg Wood

Grassy Rides -
uncommon plants
grow in the
verges & ruts.

Intake Lane

Dunnington

Woodland Flowers
most abundant in
the SW part of
the wood.

Common Road

paths

Old Sewage
Works

Hassacarr Lane

Hassacarr Pond

Alder Wood
- valuable
habitat for
a wide range
of birds.

Hagg Lane

The long history of the wood
has been researched by the
Friends of Hagg Wood from
whom copies of '**Hagg Wood -
Past & Present**' are available.

Hull Road - A1079

100m

© J. Ward 2006

Hassacarr Nature Reserve

Grid Reference: SE 672 519.   4.5 acres of which there is free public access to 3 acres.
Owned by: Dunnington Parish Council.   Managed by: Dunnington Conservation Group.

The most significant feature of Hassacarr Nature Reserve is the ancient pond, important for dragonflies and water beetles.

Buses: First York service 10 and East Yorkshire service 746 stop in Dunnington village.
By Car: Take A1079 from York. Limited parking at entrance to each site.

The City Centre

The green ring of the city walls' embankments links a variety of small parks and informal green sites, with an overall area of some 40 acres. The banks of the River Ouse and River Foss are green links to the surrounding countryside, providing valuable wildlife corridors and attractive walking routes.

Yorkshire Museum Gardens
- fine trees and grassy slopes around the ruins of St. Mary's Abbey, the Yorkshire Museum and the medieval Hospitium. The gardens are a popular summer picnic spot.

Memorial Gardens
- a formal park surrounds the war memorial.

Medieval City Walls
- a walkway around most of the length of the walls offers a unique view of the historic city centre and a glimpse into hidden green spaces not open to the public. Along the moat there are many fine, mature trees, planted in the 18th and 19th centuries.

River Ouse
York's main river is a wildlife corridor through a densely built-up area. Geese and ducks flying over the city often orientate themselves along the Ouse. Footpaths along the riverside lead north to Clifton Ings and south to Rowntree Park and Fulford Ings.

Access: The City Walls have stepped access points at all bars and end towers. The walkway is not accessible to wheelchair users. Parks and Gardens shown and paths alongside the River Ouse are generally accessible, with detours available to avoid steps. Paths along the Foss are less accessible.

Bus Stops: B1 - Theatre Royal - First York 1,2,6
B2 - Museum Street - First York Park & Ride
B3 - Layerthorpe - First 6,11,12,13 & Coastliner
B4 - Ouse Bridge - First 1,2,4,6,11,13 & Coastliner

Car Parks: Charges apply. Make sure you have change for the ticket machine.

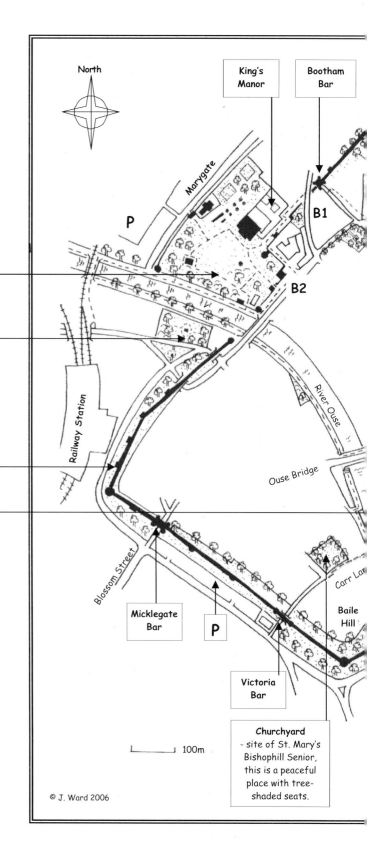

North

King's Manor

Bootham Bar

Marygate

P

B1

B2

Railway Station

River Ouse

Ouse Bridge

Blossom Street

Carr Lane

Baile Hill

Micklegate Bar

P

Victoria Bar

Churchyard
- site of St. Mary's Bishophill Senior, this is a peaceful place with tree-shaded seats.

100m

© J. Ward 2006

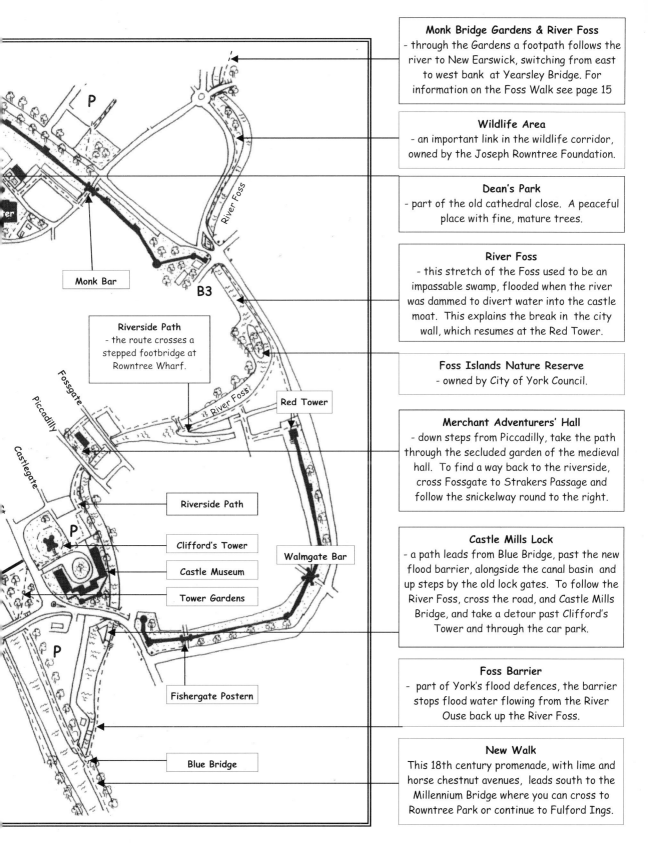

Monk Bridge Gardens & River Foss
- through the Gardens a footpath follows the river to New Earswick, switching from east to west bank at Yearsley Bridge. For information on the Foss Walk see page 15

Wildlife Area
- an important link in the wildlife corridor, owned by the Joseph Rowntree Foundation.

Dean's Park
- part of the old cathedral close. A peaceful place with fine, mature trees.

River Foss
- this stretch of the Foss used to be an impassable swamp, flooded when the river was dammed to divert water into the castle moat. This explains the break in the city wall, which resumes at the Red Tower.

Foss Islands Nature Reserve
- owned by City of York Council.

Merchant Adventurers' Hall
- down steps from Piccadilly, take the path through the secluded garden of the medieval hall. To find a way back to the riverside, cross Fossgate to Strakers Passage and follow the snickelway round to the right.

Castle Mills Lock
- a path leads from Blue Bridge, past the new flood barrier, alongside the canal basin and up steps by the old lock gates. To follow the River Foss, cross the road, and Castle Mills Bridge, and take a detour past Clifford's Tower and through the car park.

Foss Barrier
- part of York's flood defences, the barrier stops flood water flowing from the River Ouse back up the River Foss.

New Walk
This 18th century promenade, with lime and horse chestnut avenues, leads south to the Millennium Bridge where you can cross to Rowntree Park or continue to Fulford Ings.

P

Monk Bar

B3

Riverside Path
- the route crosses a stepped footbridge at Rowntree Wharf.

River Foss

River Foss

Fossgate

Piccadilly

Castlegate

Red Tower

Riverside Path

P

Clifford's Tower

Castle Museum

Tower Gardens

Walmgate Bar

P

Fishergate Postern

Blue Bridge

Green Places in South York

South York is particularly well endowed with green places, ranging from the formal gardens o Rowntree Park to the wild, marshy pasture of Fulford Ings and the sandy heathland o Heslington Common.   The Millennium Bridge links cycle and footpaths either side of the Rive Ouse offering a variety of off-road routes between different green places.

Micklegate Stray

Grid Reference: SE 593 500.   Open access, except to racecourse.   Informal paths.
Owned and managed by City of York Council.

The largest and best known of York's historic strays, Micklegate Stray is today made up of four distinct areas: Scarcroft Green, Hob Moor, Little Hob Moor and the Knavesmire, home to the city's famous racecourse.

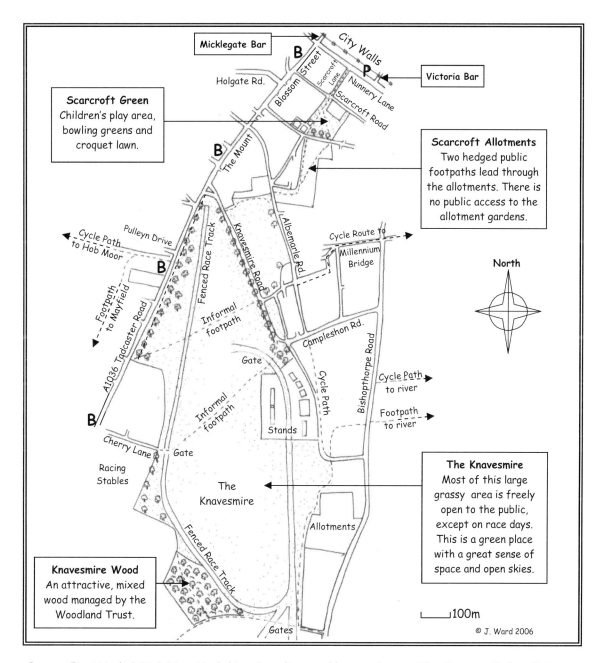

Micklegate Bar

Victoria Bar

Scarcroft Green
Children's play area, bowling greens and croquet lawn.

Scarcroft Allotments
Two hedged public footpaths lead through the allotments. There is no public access to the allotment gardens.

Holgate Rd.

Blossom Street

City Walls

Scarcroft Lane

Nunnery Lane

Scarcroft Road

The Mount

Pulleyn Drive

Cycle Path to Hob Moor

Footpath to Mayfield

A1036 Tadcaster Road

Fenced Race Track

Knavesmire Road

Albemarle Rd.

Cycle Route to Millennium Bridge

Informal footpath

Campleshon Rd.

Bishopthorpe Road

Cycle Path to river

Footpath to river

North

Gate

Cycle Path

Informal footpath

Stands

Cherry Lane

Gate

Racing Stables

The Knavesmire

Allotments

The Knavesmire
Most of this large grassy area is freely open to the public, except on race days. This is a green place with a great sense of space and open skies.

Knavesmire Wood
An attractive, mixed wood managed by the Woodland Trust.

Fenced Race Track

Gates

100m

© J. Ward 2006

Buses: First York 4,12 & 13 or Yorkshire Coastliner to Blossom Street, The Mount or Pulleyn Drive.
By Bike: Signposted route from Millennium Bridge. Cycle path around the south of the Knavesmire leads via York College to Sustrans Route 65 to Selby.
Parking: Pay & Display car park on Nunnery Lane. Limited on-street parking in Albemarle Rd. area.

Rowntree Park

Grid Reference: SE 604 507.
Open from 8.00 to dusk.

Owned and managed by City of York Council.
Easy access with mostly level paths.

A 30-acre Edwardian public park in the green corridor along the River Ouse, just south of the city centre. Easily accessible by foot or bike along the riverside or across the Millennium Bridge.

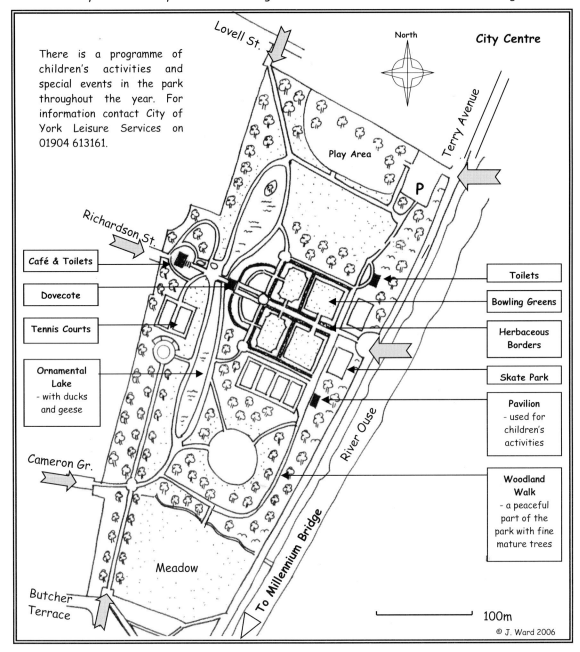

There is a programme of children's activities and special events in the park throughout the year. For information contact City of York Leisure Services on 01904 613161.

Lovell St.

North

City Centre

Terry Avenue

Play Area

P

Richardson St.

Café & Toilets

Dovecote

Tennis Courts

Ornamental Lake
- with ducks and geese

Cameron Gr.

Butcher Terrace

Meadow

To Millennium Bridge

River Ouse

Toilets

Bowling Greens

Herbaceous Borders

Skate Park

Pavilion
- used for children's activities

Woodland Walk
- a peaceful part of the park with fine mature trees

100m

© J. Ward 2006

Buses: First York 11 to Bishopthorpe Road, then follow signs down Butcher Terrace to Millennium Bridge. The Park is on the left.
By Car: Small car park at park entrance with access from Terry Avenue.

Danesmead Meadow

Grid Reference: SE 605 498.   Owned by YNET.   Managed by Danesmead Meadow Association.

This small, community wildlife site includes a pond, wild flower meadow and community orchard. The orchard was planted in memory of English Nature officer, Shona Matheson, with 22 apple varieties, including local rarities.   The meadow hosts regular community events.   Open Access.

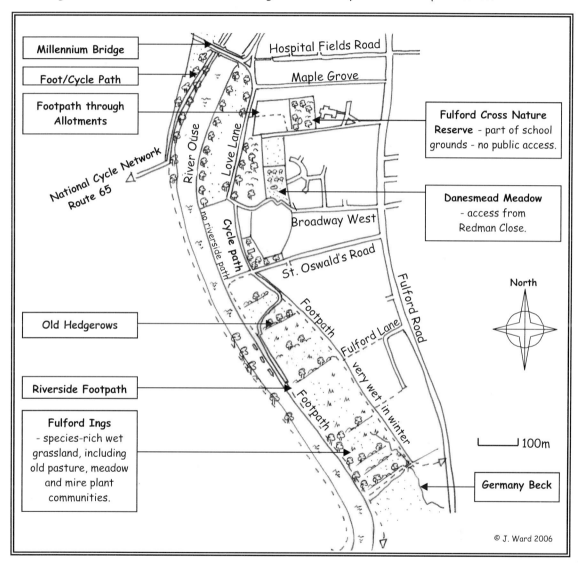

Millennium Bridge

Foot/Cycle Path

Footpath through Allotments

National Cycle Network Route 65

River Ouse

Love Lane

Hospital Fields Road

Maple Grove

Fulford Cross Nature Reserve - part of school grounds - no public access.

Danesmead Meadow - access from Redman Close.

Broadway West

Cycle path

no riverside path

St. Oswald's Road

Old Hedgerows

Riverside Footpath

Fulford Ings - species-rich wet grassland, including old pasture, meadow and mire plant communities.

Footpath

Footpath

Fulford Lane

very wet in winter

Fulford Road

North

100m

Germany Beck

© J. Ward 2006

Fulford Ings

Grid Reference: SE 608 491   Open Access.   May be flooded in winter. Some paths wet all year.

Designated a Site of Special Scientific Interest (SSSI) as an example of flood plain mire, the Ings offer a great sense of space and plenty of botanical interest. Beautiful in early summer when great swathes of pink bistort and yellow buttercups are in flower.

Bus: First York Service 7 runs regularly along Fulford Road.

Walmgate Stray

Grid Reference: SE 616 504.   Open Access.   Informal paths, wet & muddy in winter.
Managed by City of York Council in consultation with Freemen of the City.

Cattle still graze the low, marshy grassland of this stray - a remnant of York's historic landscape.

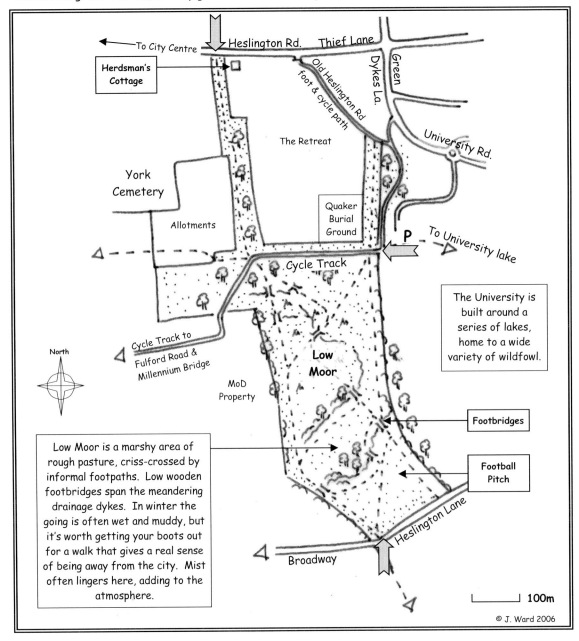

To City Centre

Herdsman's Cottage

Heslington Rd.   Thief Lane

Old Heslington Rd
foot & cycle path

Dykes La.

Green

University Rd.

The Retreat

York Cemetery

Allotments

Quaker Burial Ground

P

To University lake

Cycle Track

The University is built around a series of lakes, home to a wide variety of wildfowl.

North

Cycle Track to Fulford Road & Millennium Bridge

Low Moor

MoD Property

Footbridges

Football Pitch

Low Moor is a marshy area of rough pasture, criss-crossed by informal footpaths. Low wooden footbridges span the meandering drainage dykes. In winter the going is often wet and muddy, but it's worth getting your boots out for a walk that gives a real sense of being away from the city. Mist often lingers here, adding to the atmosphere.

Broadway

Heslington Lane

100m

© J. Ward 2006

Walmgate Stray is shielded from traffic noise and enhanced by mature trees in the neighbouring grounds of The Retreat and York University. The university grounds are open to the public.

Bus: First York 4 to Heslington Rd. or University Rd.   **Parking:** Pay & Display on university campus.

Heslington Common, West Moor & Tillmire

Grid Reference: SE 635 481 (Heslington Common) / SE 625 490 (West Moor) / SE 636 476

Ancient pathways link areas of moor, mire and heathland that were once common grazing for the village of Heslington.   West Moor and Heslington Common are now leased by Fulford Golf Club. Although there is no public access to the land, public footpaths leading across the moor and round the common give good views of the varied habitats.

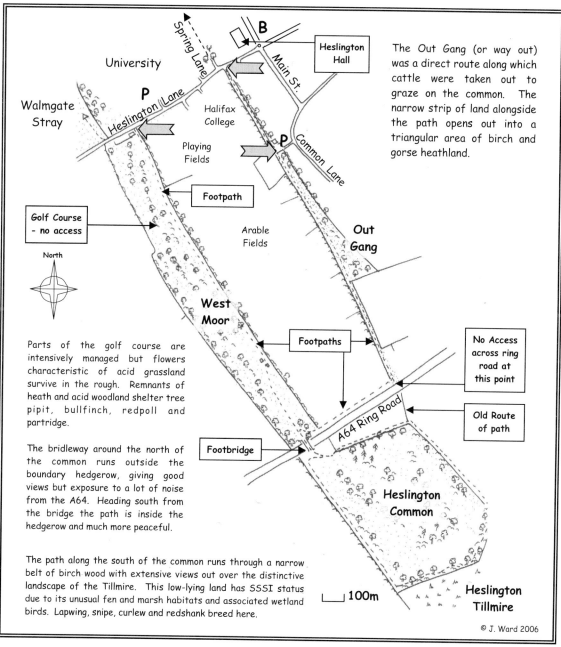

University

Walmgate Stray

Spring Lane

Heslington Lane

P

B

Main St.

Heslington Hall

Halifax College

Playing Fields

Common Lane

Footpath

Golf Course - no access

North

Arable Fields

Out Gang

West Moor

Footpaths

No Access across ring road at this point

Old Route of path

A64 Ring Road

Footbridge

Heslington Common

Heslington Tillmire

The Out Gang (or way out) was a direct route along which cattle were taken out to graze on the common.   The narrow strip of land alongside the path opens out into a triangular area of birch and gorse heathland.

Parts of the golf course are intensively managed but flowers characteristic of acid grassland survive in the rough. Remnants of heath and acid woodland shelter tree pipit, bullfinch, redpoll and partridge.

The bridleway around the north of the common runs outside the boundary hedgerow, giving good views but exposure to a lot of noise from the A64. Heading south from the bridge the path is inside the hedgerow and much more peaceful.

The path along the south of the common runs through a narrow belt of birch wood with extensive views out over the distinctive landscape of the Tillmire. This low-lying land has SSSI status due to its unusual fen and marsh habitats and associated wetland birds. Lapwing, snipe, curlew and redshank breed here.

100m

© J. Ward 2006

Bus: First York 4 to Heslington Hall.   **Parking:** Pay & Display on university campus.

York Cemetery

Grid Reference: SE 613 508.
Open from 9.00 to dusk daily.

Owned and Managed by York Cemetery Trust.
Easy access with mostly level pathways.

A Victorian cemetery, with later extension, managed on ecological principles.   24 acres.

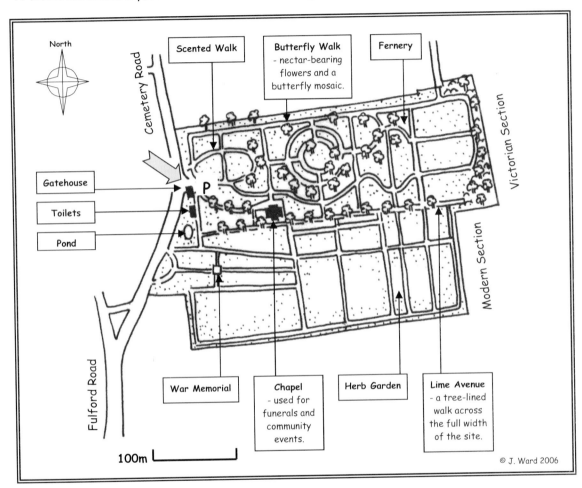

North

Cemetery Road

Scented Walk

Butterfly Walk
- nectar-bearing
flowers and a
butterfly mosaic.

Fernery

Victorian Section

Gatehouse

Toilets

Pond

P

Modern Section

Fulford Road

War Memorial

Chapel
- used for
funerals and
community
events.

Herb Garden

Lime Avenue
- a tree-lined
walk across
the full width
of the site.

100m

© J. Ward 2006

High walls and mature trees contribute to the peaceful and secluded atmosphere. This is a very special place, for people and for wildlife. York Cemetery Trust, through the work of their warden and volunteers, manages the site in a way which balances the needs of bereaved families with the ecological management of a diverse site. Some areas are planted with ornamental species, chosen for scent, colour and wildlife benefit. In other parts the semi-natural vegetation is allowed to develop within boundaries set by mown pathways.   The site is a haven for many species of invertebrates, birds and small mammals.

For information on guided walks and special events, contact the warden on 01904 610578.

Bus: Arriva 415, First York 7, Top Line Travel 128 to Fulford Road / Cemetery Road.

Wheldrake Ings

Grid Reference: SE 694 444.   Owned and Managed by: Yorkshire Wildlife Trust.
Part of the Lower Derwent Valley National Nature Reserve. No dogs or bicycles allowed on reserve.

Over 150 hectares of alluvial flood meadow, internationally important for its rich hay meadow flora and the waders and wildfowl which winter on the seasonal wetland. A wild and beautiful place.

Visitors are asked to keep to the footpaths leading to the hides.

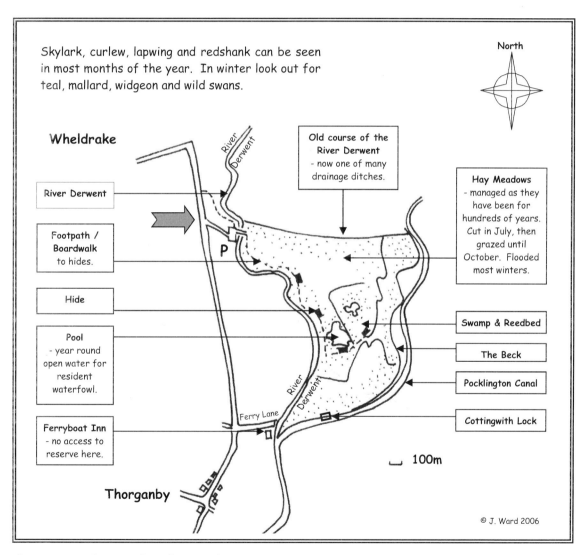

Skylark, curlew, lapwing and redshank can be seen in most months of the year. In winter look out for teal, mallard, widgeon and wild swans.

North

Wheldrake

River Derwent

Old course of the River Derwent
- now one of many drainage ditches.

Hay Meadows
- managed as they have been for hundreds of years. Cut in July, then grazed until October. Flooded most winters.

River Derwent

Footpath / Boardwalk
to hides.

P

Hide

Swamp & Reedbed

The Beck

Pool
- year round open water for resident waterfowl.

Pocklington Canal

River Derwent

Ferry Lane

Cottingwith Lock

Ferryboat Inn
- no access to reserve here.

100m

Thorganby

© J. Ward 2006

Buses: First York 18 from York City Centre passes the site.
By Bike: Sustrans route 6 (York/Selby) to Escrick access; from Escrick follow Wheldrake Lane.
By Car   Take the A19 south from York. Turn left at Crockey Hill to Wheldrake.
              Limited parking at Reserve entrance.

Green Places in West York

The area west of the main railway line and south of the River Ouse includes some of York's bes
hidden green places. You have to make an effort to find some of them, but you may be rewarde
by unexpected bird song or surprising peace and quiet.

Acomb Wood

Grid reference: SE 560494   Open Access.   Level paths through main woodland area.
Owned & managed by City of York Council (East Wood) & Woodland Trust (West Wood).

Ten acres of mixed woodland and an ancient meadow.

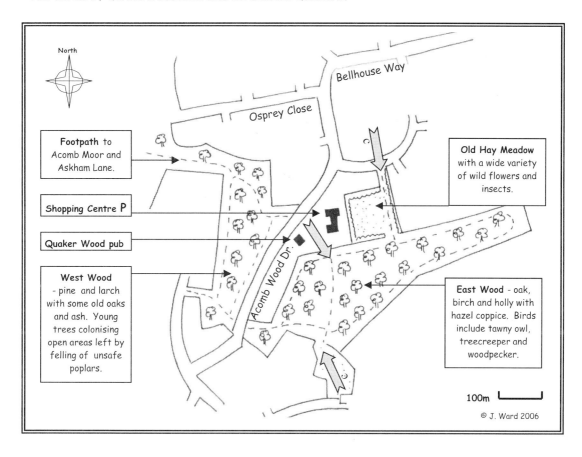

Bellhouse Way

Osprey Close

North

Footpath to Acomb Moor and Askham Lane.

Shopping Centre P

Quaker Wood pub

West Wood
- pine and larch with some old oaks and ash. Young trees colonising open areas left by felling of unsafe poplars.

Acomb Wood Dr.

Old Hay Meadow with a wide variety of wild flowers and insects.

East Wood - oak, birch and holly with hazel coppice. Birds include tawny owl, treecreeper and woodpecker.

100m

© J. Ward 2006

Acomb Wood is a green oasis in the middle of a large housing estate. Both parts of the wood have had a chequered history with plantation planting and periods of neglect. Old ridge and furrow in the east wood suggest this area was planted with trees in the 18th century, after a time as arable fields. Uncommon woodland wild flowers in the west wood, including sanicle and twayblade, suggest this is an ancient woodland site.

The woodland, meadow and surrounding hedgerows provide habitat for a wide range of birds, small mammals and invertebrates. Great spotted woodpecker, treecreeper and nuthatch nest in holes in the old trees. Coal tit and long-tailed tit feed in the treetops. Robin, thrush and willow warbler sing in the hedgerows. Butterflies seen in the meadow include Small Skipper, Common Blue and Small Copper.

Bus: First York no. 4 to Foxwood Lane shops. Follow Bellhouse Way to Acomb Wood Drive.
Car park: At the shopping centre on Acomb Wood Drive.
Toilets: For customers at the Quaker Wood pub.

Askham Bog Nature Reserve

Grid Reference: SE 575 481.   Owned and Managed by Yorkshire Wildlife Trust.

Open access to boardwalk trail.   Dogs must be kept under close control.

Askham Bog is a remnant of the ancient valley mire which once stretched over large parts of the Vale of York. Over the centuries small-scale peat cutting, grazing and timber production have led to the development of a succession of fen and carr (marsh woodland) habitats. The varied habitats support over 300 plant species and a huge variety of insects, including many rarities. Among the birds which breed here are woodcock, reed warbler and lesser spotted woodpecker. Redpoll and siskin are winter visitors. Roe deer can occasionally be seen grazing in the woodland glades.

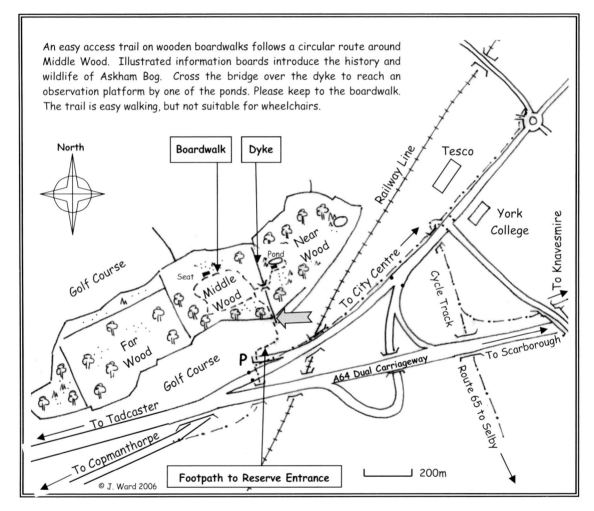

An easy access trail on wooden boardwalks follows a circular route around Middle Wood. Illustrated information boards introduce the history and wildlife of Askham Bog. Cross the bridge over the dyke to reach an observation platform by one of the ponds. Please keep to the boardwalk. The trail is easy walking, but not suitable for wheelchairs.

© J. Ward 2006

The background noise from the dual carriageway and railway doesn't seem to bother the wildlife. After a while you'll probably find you can ignore it too. Askham Bog is a surprisingly tranquil place.

By Bike: For an off-road route take Cycle Route 65 out of York along the river and follow signs to the Knavesmire. Cross Sim Balk Lane and Tadcaster Road under the bridges, then follow the road-side cycle path over the railway to the reserve slip road.   **Nearest Bus Stop:** York College.

By Car: Take the A1036 Tadcaster Road out of York. At lights, turn right towards Copmanthorpe. Look out for the bridge over the railway. The access road to the reserve is straight after the bridge, before the next traffic lights.

Bachelor Hill

Grid Reference: SE 572 513.   Open Access.   Owned and Managed by City of York Council.
No paths, but easy walking on well-drained grass.   Not wheelchair accessible.

A well-hidden site, worth seeking out, Bachelor Hill offers an unrivalled panoramic view across the city to the Yorkshire Wolds and North York Moors. Entering the site from Askham Lane brings you to the top of the sandy knoll with very little climbing.   Grassy slopes, a hill top copse of pine and horse chestnut trees and an old sand pit make this an attractive place for a picnic. The rough grassland of the unusual 'sand dune' is habitat for many different butterfly species.

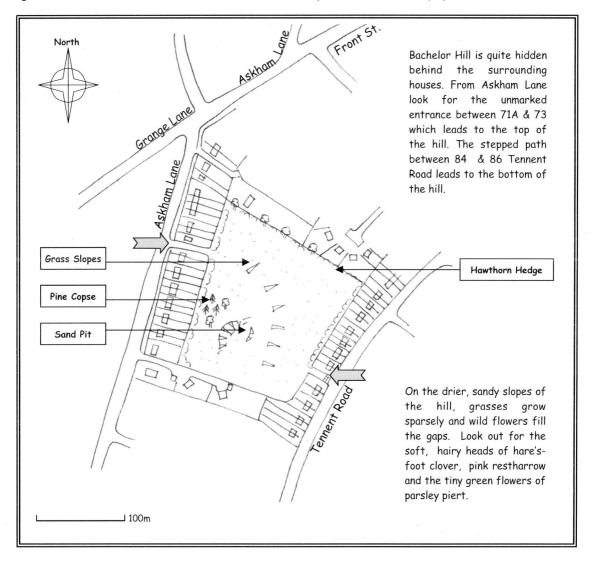

North

Bachelor Hill is quite hidden behind the surrounding houses. From Askham Lane look for the unmarked entrance between 71A & 73 which leads to the top of the hill. The stepped path between 84 & 86 Tennent Road leads to the bottom of the hill.

Grass Slopes

Pine Copse

Sand Pit

Hawthorn Hedge

On the drier, sandy slopes of the hill, grasses grow sparsely and wild flowers fill the gaps. Look out for the soft, hairy heads of hare's-foot clover, pink restharrow and the tiny green flowers of parsley piert.

100m

Buses: First York 1 runs frequently the City Centre to Acomb Green, then 500m walk along Askham Lane, or First York 26 hourly to Front Street.

Parking: On-street parking on Askham Lane.

Chapman's Pond

Grid Reference: SE 578 491.   Open Access.   Main path surfaced, others muddy in winter.
Owned by City of York Council.   Managed by CoYC assisted by Friends of Chapman's Pond.

A flooded brick pit, and adjacent scrub woodland. This small site is a valuable feeding ground for waterfowl and song-birds. Coot, moorhen and mallard nest here and tufted ducks are winter visitors. The pond has been stocked with a variety of coarse fish and is used for angling.

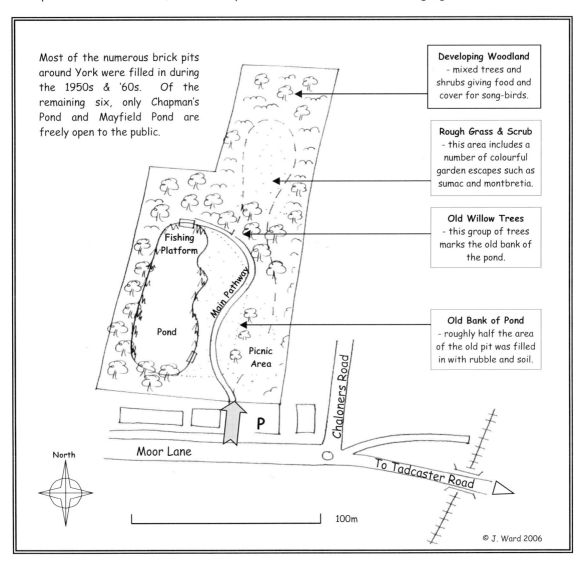

Most of the numerous brick pits around York were filled in during the 1950s & '60s. Of the remaining six, only Chapman's Pond and Mayfield Pond are freely open to the public.

Developing Woodland - mixed trees and shrubs giving food and cover for song-birds.

Rough Grass & Scrub - this area includes a number of colourful garden escapes such as sumac and montbretia.

Old Willow Trees - this group of trees marks the old bank of the pond.

Old Bank of Pond - roughly half the area of the old pit was filled in with rubble and soil.

Fishing Platform

Pond

Main Pathway

Picnic Area

Chaloners Road

Moor Lane

To Tadcaster Road

P

North

100m

© J. Ward 2006

Bus: First York Service 12 from City Centre to Moor Lane.

Parking: Space for six cars at site entrance.

Fishponds Wood and Beech Grove, Acomb

Grid Reference: SE 575 517 (Fishponds Wood).   Open Access.   Level Paths.
Owned by: City of York Council.   Managed by: CoYC in consultation with Friends groups.

Two small sites with fine mature beech trees and young trees planted by local residents.

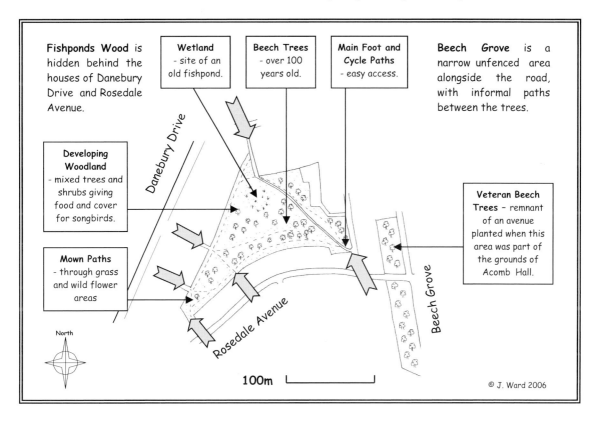

Fishponds Wood is hidden behind the houses of Danebury Drive and Rosedale Avenue.

Wetland - site of an old fishpond.

Beech Trees - over 100 years old.

Main Foot and Cycle Paths - easy access.

Beech Grove is a narrow unfenced area alongside the road, with informal paths between the trees.

Developing Woodland - mixed trees and shrubs giving food and cover for songbirds.

Mown Paths - through grass and wild flower areas

Veteran Beech Trees – remnant of an avenue planted when this area was part of the grounds of Acomb Hall.

Danebury Drive

Rosedale Avenue

Beech Grove

North

100m

© J. Ward 2006

Bus: First York no.1 from City Centre to Acomb Shops. Beech Grove is a turning by the Health Centre - foot and cycle access only from this end.
Parking: On-street parking is not restricted on Rosedale Avenue, Beech Grove & Danebury Drive.

Other Green Sites in Acomb

From SW corner of Fishponds Wood, cross Rosedale Avenue to reach **St. Stephen's Churchyard.** The path through the churchyard leads past the church, via a steep path and steps, to **Acomb Green.** The churchyard has some fine mature trees. The Green is mostly mown grass, with steep banks (the legacy of excavations for building sand) and a few groups of trees.   Neither the churchyard nor the Green have particular wildlife interest, but both are significant features in the historic landscape of Acomb - reminders of the days when this was a rural village.

From the SW corner of the Green a 500 metre walk along Askham Lane takes you to **Bachelor Hill.** For details of this well-hidden site, see page 37.

Hob Moor Local Nature Reserve

Grid Reference: SE 585 505.   Open Access.   Foot/cycle path surfaced, others informal.
Owned by City of York Council.   Managed in consultation with Friends of Hob Moor & English Nature.

One of the ancient commons of York and part of Micklegate Stray, Hob Moor is now a designated Local Nature Reserve. 89 acres of mostly open grassland with a great sense of space, good views to York Minster and the chance to enjoy the song of skylarks.

For more on history and wildlife, see 'Hob Moor: Historic Stray and Local Nature Reserve', published by Sessions of York.

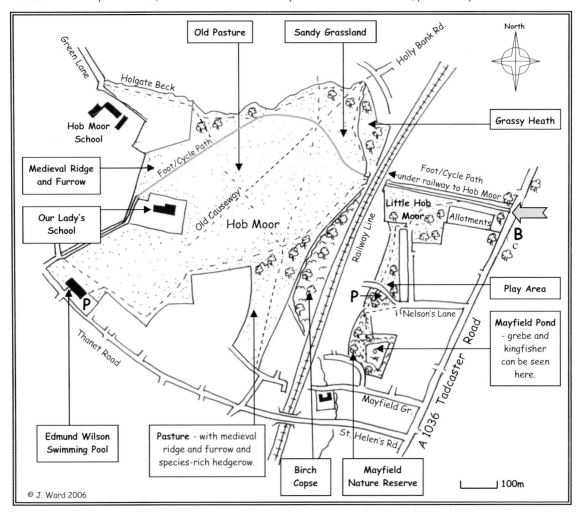

© J. Ward 2006

Mayfield Nature Reserve

Grid Reference: SE 587 503   Managed jointly by YNET and Friends of Mayfield Nature Reserve.

An old brick pit, surrounded by a small birch and willow wood. The pond has a well-established ecosystem and a good range of fish. Day tickets for angling are available from the bailiff on the bank.
Access from Little Hob Moor (which adjoins the north part of the reserve), from Mayfield Grove or from Nelson's Lane, where there is a small car park.

Buses: First York 4 & 13 and Yorkshire Coastliner to Tadcaster Road. Ask for the Pulleyn Drive stop.

West Bank Park

Grid Reference: SE 585 513   Owned and managed by City of York Council.
Open from 8.00 to dusk.   Easy access except stepped rose garden and woodland path.

The fine mature trees of this 20-acre park date from the 19th century when this site was the Backhouse Nursery and the gardens of its owner's home, West Bank House. Today rose gardens, bowling greens and clipped hedges contrast with wild flower meadows and informal woodland areas.

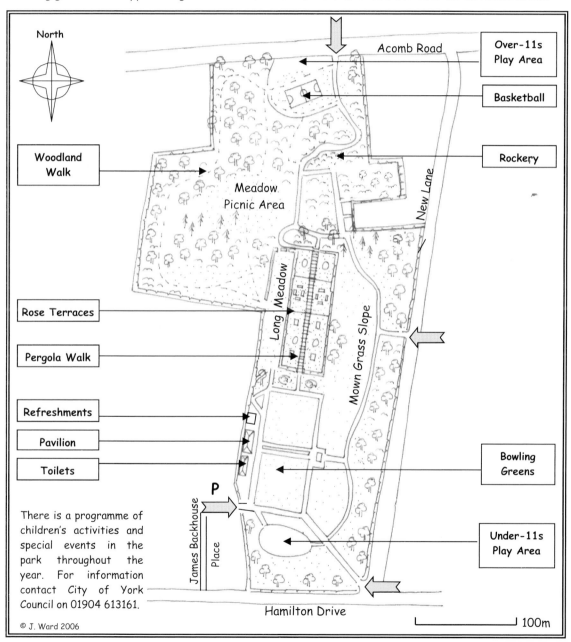

© J. Ward 2006

Buses: First York 1 frequently from city centre to Acomb Road, stops by park gates.

Parking: On-street parking on New Lane or Hamilton Drive.

Wheatlands Community Woodland

Grid Reference: SE 562 530

Owned by Mr and Mrs B. Otley.   Managed by Wheatlands Woodland Group.   Open Access.

A newly-planted wood with a developing range of wildlife habitats.
Illustrated information boards & trail leaflets available on the site.

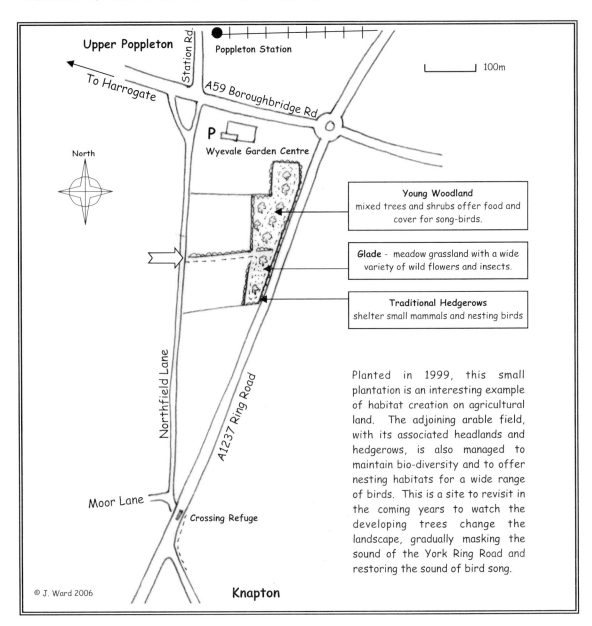

Upper Poppleton

Poppleton Station

Station Rd.

To Harrogate

A59 Boroughbridge Rd

100m

P

Wyevale Garden Centre

North

Young Woodland
mixed trees and shrubs offer food and
cover for song-birds.

Glade - meadow grassland with a wide
variety of wild flowers and insects.

Traditional Hedgerows
shelter small mammals and nesting birds

Northfield Lane

A1237 Ring Road

Moor Lane

Crossing Refuge

Planted in 1999, this small plantation is an interesting example of habitat creation on agricultural land. The adjoining arable field, with its associated headlands and hedgerows, is also managed to maintain bio-diversity and to offer nesting habitats for a wide range of birds. This is a site to revisit in the coming years to watch the developing trees change the landscape, gradually masking the sound of the York Ring Road and restoring the sound of bird song.

© J. Ward 2006

Knapton

Buses: First York service 10 to Station Road / A59 junction.
Train: Services from York to Harrogate stop at Poppleton, a half-mile walk from Wheatlands.
By Bike: For a quiet route from Acomb, take Knapton Lane & Ten Thorn Lane to Knapton Main Street. When you reach the A1237 turn right along the short stretch of cycle path to the crossing refuge. Once safely across the main road, a gate leads you into the quieter Northfield Lane.
By Car: Take A59 Boroughbridge Rd. to turning by Wyevale Garden Centre.

What Next?

This guide is inevitably incomplete. We hope it will inspire you to explore the green places of York, branching out from the sites and routes described to find special places of your own. If you are planning walks or bike rides linking two or more green places, you'll find one of the maps listed below helpful. The selection of books, reports and web sites listed includes some used in the preparation of this guide and others that give background information on individual sites or ideas for further walks.

The information in this guide is correct to the best of our knowledge and information at the time of publication. Comments, corrections or suggestions for inclusion in any future editions can be sent to Sessions Book Trust, The Ebor Press, York YO31 9HS.

Maps

Ordnance Survey Explorer™ 290
1:25,000 scale map showing public rights of way.
Particularly useful for finding public footpaths and cycle routes linking green places in the outskirts of the city and surrounding countryside.

PHOTOMAP™ of York
Published by Overview Mapping Ltd.
A street map overlaid on an aerial photo, taken in 1999 as part of the first complete aerial survey of the United Kingdom. The unique view of York's green places offered by this map was invaluable in the preparation of this guide. Good for finding your way, too.

York Cycle Route Map
Published by City of York Council
Available free of charge from libraries and tourist information offices.

Books & Reports

Beyond the Bars: Ten Walks from York City Walls, by Ivan Broadhead
Published by Meridian Books, Oldbury, 1989
ISBN 1869922050, 192pp
A detailed guide to ten circular walks of between 2 and 7 miles, starting from the historic gateways of the Bar Walls and exploring green places in the suburbs and villages of York.

City of York Biodiversity Audit, by Martin Hammond, Ecological Consultant, 1996
In the preparation of the guide the author referred many times to this unpublished report, prepared for City of York Council and English Nature.

The Foss Walk by Mark Jones
Published by Maxiprint, York, 1989
14pp, illustrated with maps and line drawings, ISBN 1871125014,
This pocket-sized booklet will help you find your way from Easingwold to the source of the River Foss at Pond Head, between the villages of Oulston and Yearsley, then downstream to the Foss outflow to the River Ouse, by Blue Bridge in York.

The River Foss - Its History and Natural History by Michael Fife & Peter Walls
Published by William Sessions Ltd., The Ebor Press, York, 1981
68pp, ISBN 0 900657 17 0
A illustrated history of the River Foss, including its canalization to Sheriff Hutton Bridge in the 1790s, followed by wildlife narrative and species lists. Also included are two pages showing the complete River Foss Walk, from Pond Head to Castle Mills Lock in York and suggestions for six shorter walks along the downstream sections of the river.

The Complete Snickelways of York by Mark Jones
Published by Maxiprint, York, 1991
172pp, ISBN 1 871125 04 9
Many hidden green places appear in the line drawings and colour photos of this guide to the snickets, ginnels and alleyways of central York.

The Strays and Ways of York by the York Group for the Promotion of Planning
Published by Sessions Book Trust, York, 1968, 44pp
If you'd like more information on the history of York's strays and other green sites, this is a good place to start. Produced by a group keen to ensure that the strays and other green sites of York were protected from development - still a live issue. York has changed and grown a lot since 1968, so this guide is of historic interest in its own right now.

Web Sites

In addition to the web sites mentioned in the introduction:

www.yorkstories.co.uk
See page 46 for a sample of photos from this site. The York Walks pages on Yorkstories offer a personal view of some of the lesser known parts of the city, focussing on natural and human details and seasonal changes. It's an eye-opening and inspiring site.

www.bbc/northyorkshire
At the time of writing this site features a web log of seasonal change at Rawcliffe Meadows and an audio walk around the meadows. By the time you read this the content may have changed, but it's worth a look.

www.thisisyork.co.uk
This local news website includes a guided walk around the City Walls. Look for it on the Tourism pages, not under Country Walks. The Communigate page gives links to the web sites of a number of green place Friends groups.

Rowntree Park attracts large numbers of people for summer picnics and special events but it has quiet corners too.

Dean's Park is a peaceful green place, hidden behind the Minster in the heart of the city.

The Minster can be glimpsed from green places all over the city. Here it is seen from St. Nicholas Field's, beyond the old incinerator chimney.

The slopes outside of the bar walls give a spectacular display of daffodils each spring. A surprising variety of wild flowers thrive on the inside banks.

Photos: Dean's Park & St. Nicks, Judith Ward; Rowntree Park & City Walls, City of York Council.

Rawcliffe Meadows in summer sunshine

Autumn flood on Rawcliffe meadows

Sheep grazing on riverside pasture at Nun Ings, just south of the Millennium Bridge

The new copse on the cycle track alongside Rawcliffe Bar Country Park

The Lime Walk (above) and some natural details (below) in York Cemetery

A peaceful picnic spot in Homestead Park

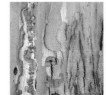

Centre right photo above by Mick Phythian. All other photos on this page by Lisa from www.yorkstories.co.uk.

AND NOW IT IS TIME TO BE OUT AND ABOUT

The Sessions Book Trust is very pleased to publish this series of 'Green' Maps, so excellently drawn and captioned by Mrs Judith Ward, because many York readers need to have these clear details about our green treasures, inviting health-giving family recreation and encouragement of ecological bio-diversity. And how about visiting at different times of the year: for spring foliage and again for autumn fungi?

The very first publication of our little family book trust was a forerunner publication to this, in 1968: a 44 page booklet entitled *The Strays and Ways of York.* This contained large maps of these 'green lungs' with which York has long been blessed: Bootham Stray, Monk Stray, Walmgate Stray as well as Knavesmire (now of 'Ascot' fame) and adjoining Hob Moor.

This new publication again includes up-dated maps of all the above-mentioned historic Strays of York, now supported and enhanced by numerous additional green places, some well-known, yet with others little known to York residents – until now. For example can you find an entrance to Clifton Backies? Or to all the entrances to Saint Nicholas Fields? You can once you have bought this booklet.

Our congratulations to Judith Ward for her skilful map-making; our thanks for the dedication of the many local management groups of these individual green areas; and now it is time for you and your family to choose one of these maps: and to be up and away to renew or to make your acquaintance with one of these many cherished green places in and around our lovely City of York.

Bill Sessions (Chairman Sessions Book Trust)